THE
CHILD'S FIRST STEPS

IN

Pianoforte Playing

BY

TOBIAS MATTHAY

(Professor, Lecturer and Fellow of the Royal Academy of Music, and Founder of the
Tobias Matthay Pianoforte School, London, etc.)

Price 3/- Net

JOSEPH WILLIAMS (LIMITED)
32 GREAT PORTLAND STREET, LONDON, W.

Read & Co.

Copyright © 2021 Read & Co. Books

This edition is published by Read & Co. Books,
an imprint of Read & Co.

This book is copyright and may not be reproduced or copied in any
way without the express permission of the publisher in writing.

British Library Cataloguing-in-Publication Data
A catalogue record for this book is available
from the British Library.

Read & Co. is part of Read Books Ltd.
For more information visit
www.readandcobooks.co.uk

Tobias Matthay

Tobias Augustus Matthay was born on 19th February 1858, in Clapham, Surrey, England. He was an English pianist, teacher and composer.

Matthay's parents originally came from northern Germany and eventually became naturalised British subjects. He studied composition at the 'Royal Academy of Music' (London) under Sir William Sterndale Bennett and Arthur Sullivan, and piano with William Dorrell and Walter Macfarren. Matthay served as a sub-professor there from 1876 to 1880, and became an assistant professor of pianoforte in 1880, before being promoted to professor in 1884.

Alongside Frederick Corder and John Blackwood McEwen (both composers and music teachers), he founded the Society of British Composers in 1905. This organisation was established with the aim of protecting the interests of British composers and to provide publication, promotion and performance opportunities. It was disbanded thirteen years later, in 1918. Matthay remained at the Royal Academy of Music until 1925, when he was forced to resign because McEwen – his former student who was then the Academy's Principal – publicly attacked his teaching.

In 1903, after over a decade of observation, analysis, and experimentation, Matthay published *The Act of Touch*, an encyclopaedic volume that influenced piano pedagogy throughout the English-speaking world. So many students were soon in quest of his insights that two years later he opened the Tobias Matthay Pianoforte School, first in Oxford Street, then in 1909 relocating to Wimpole Street, where it remained for the next thirty years. He soon became known for his teaching principles that stressed proper piano touch and analysis of arm movements. He wrote several additional books on piano technique that brought him international recognition, and in 1912 he published *Musical Interpretation*, a widely read book that analyzed the principles of effective musicianship.

Many of Matthay's pupils went on to define a school of twentieth century English pianism, including York Bowen, Myra Hess, Clifford Curzon, Moura Lympany, Eunice Norton, Lytle Powell, Irene Scharrer, Lilias Mackinnon, Guy Jonson, Vivian Langrish and Harriet Cohen. He was also the teacher of Canadian pianist Harry Dean, English composer Arnold Bax and English conductor Ernest Read.

In his private life, Matthay married Jessie (née Kennedy) in 1893, the sister of Marjory Kennedy-Fraser (the Scottish singer, composer and arranger). She sadly died in 1937.

Tobias Matthay died at his country home, High Marley, near Haslemere, on 15th December 1945. He was eighty-seven years old.

THE
CHILD'S · FIRST STEPS
IN
PIANOFORTE PLAYING

BY

TOBIAS MATTHAY

Preamble: This little work is intended for the use of the Child, or Adult Beginner, and is quite complete in itself. It would be well, however, if the *Teacher* were familiar with the *first* and *last* chapters of the author's "*First Principles of Pianoforte Playing*" (Longmans, Green & Co.); also, later on, with its Supplement, "*Some Commentaries on Pianoforte Playing*"; while some of the additional teaching-material may be found in the "*Relaxation Studies*" (Bosworth & Co.), and "*The Forearm Rotation Principle and its Mastery*" (Joseph Williams and The Boston Music Co.). and "*Musical Interpretation*," its laws and principles (Joseph Williams) †

Foreword: Before you begin to make Music on the Piano, you must already have learnt to feel the pulse of musical rhythm, and to hear the intervals of the musical scale.*

And now that you are ready to begin to make music with your own fingers on the keyboard, I will try to show you how to do this and how to understand the First Principles of Technique.

Before, however, you take the very first step in Tone-production, be sure to understand that you must never touch the Piano without *always trying to make music*. It is only too easy to sound notes without really making music at all. To make music we must make all the sounds *mean* something — just as it is of no use pretending to speak unless the sounds we make with our lips mean something, that is, unless they form reasoned phrases and sentences.

* This preliminary education may be carried out on the lines of Mrs. Spencer Curwen's admirable "*Child Pianist,*" or other work of similar scope.

And how can we make a series of musical sounds "mean something"? We shall learn to do this if we try to see that there is no music without a reasoned rhythm, and that such rhythm implies always a definite Progression or Movement. We must learn, then, from the first, as Pianists, to feel that all the notes we play, or hear, *are going somewhere,* — are *moving* towards a climax; that they lead onwards towards a rhythmical goal, a Pulse (or beat), or some other more important musical *landmark.* We must learn to feel pulse itself and its divisions as being a Progression, and must learn *at all times* to fit the notes we play into such pulse-progressions or recurring Time-throbs. For instance:

Ex. No. 1

And we must learn to see how such pulse-progressions lead us further and further on as they grow into little phrases, large phrases, sentences, and

† The Music Material for use with this work is to be found in "*The Pianist's First Music Making,*" by TOBIAS MATTHAY and FELIX SWINSTEAD, issued by The Anglo-French Music Co., London.

Ex. No. 2

through bigger climaxes into a complete piece — a short Tune or a long Movement (Exercise No. 2).

We perceive Progression in Music (*i.e.*, its Shape) through the ear, just as we perceive the shape of the *progressions* of the lines in drawing or writing through the eye. Presently, if you try to understand Music, you will find things there which are far more interesting even than its Shapes, for you will find that all real Music is meant to *say something to you* — that it is meant to express FEELING.

In short: Remember that every sound you make must be part of a musical Progression or *shape*, and, besides this, that there is always a *mood* to be expressed.*

But before you may touch the Piano, you still have to learn to understand Step I.

Step I: Your teacher will open the Piano, so that you can see its *action* or mechanism. Notice, when you move a key down, that its little *hammer* moves against its own set of strings, and then at once *flies back*. Notice how the strings continue sounding while the key is kept down, although the hammer remains away from the strings. From this you learn that you really make the sound just before and up to the beginning of it, for it is by *moving* the key down that you make

* The author has been the first to point out that Shape, Rhythm and Phrasing in Music imply *Movement* in this sense, and he gladly welcomes the acceptance of his views on this point by some of our more up-to-date teachers of theory.

the hammer hit the strings. Also you learn that you can do nothing to alter the *sound* once the key is down, since the hammer flies back as soon as you reach the sound in key-descent. But if you hold the key down (gently) the strings continue to sound (more and more faintly) until you let the key rise, when the sound at once stops. Notice that the sound stops, because a *damper* falls upon the strings when you allow the key to rise. This "damper" you had raised from the strings when you pressed the key down, and you kept it raised off the strings so long as you kept the key down.*

You have now learnt that you *make* the sound at the very beginning of it, as you move the key down, and that it is useless to squeeze the key upon the pad (or "bed") beneath it for that purpose; and that to do this will only hinder you in your playing. Remember, the only way to make a sound is *to make the key move;* and you will find that *the quicker* you make the key move the *louder* is the sound.

* If you press the right Pedal down, *all* the dampers are thereby raised from the strings, so that any strings you may then sound will continue sounding until you let the Pedal rise again.

You must now prove this to yourself by trying experiments with the keys. That is, move a key down repeatedly and try to make the *movement* each time quicker and quicker; and if you really succeed in making the key move down quicker and quicker, you will hear that the sound is each time louder and louder. Listen most carefully all the time. Next, try to move it down rather slower, and the sound will then be softer, and if you are careful you can move it slower and slower until you succeed in making it very soft.

You feel now what makes the difference between loud and soft. You also see how careful you must always be to try to make this movement of the key *before it is too late to make it.* For if you try *too late* to make the full speed of the key, you will only fix the key upon its bed *before* you have made the sound you meant to make. And, if the sounds are not just what you meant to make, the result *cannot be music.*

It comes to this: that you must always exactly *time* the moment you want each note to *begin* sounding; that is, you must be careful to see that you *finish* moving the key just at that very moment. Experiment again and again, and listen most carefully all the time, so that you may thoroughly understand these points, (*a*) so that you may apply the necessary force *early enough* during the descent of the key, and (*b*) so that you may learn accurately to *time* the beginning of each sound.

Step II: Now remember, *unless each note sounds just the right loudness,* your piece cannot possibly sound rightly, musically. Therefore the next step is that you must learn to tell *how much* muscular force will be required for each note; that is, the *least possible* amount of force that will make it sound rightly. Now, in trying your last experiments you will have noticed that it requires *more force* to move the key quickly than to move it slowly, although the loudest note requires *far less force* than you would at first expect — provided you apply the force *early enough* in key-descent. Notice again, but still more carefully this time, what happens when you put the key down slowly, and then quickly, and you will find that the key *resists you more* the quicker you try to move it — that is, it *feels more difficult to move* it quickly than slowly. And although (even for a very loud note) its greatest resistance against your finger is not very great, you can, all the same, feel that the resistance, as the key goes down, is greater or less as the tone is louder or softer.

To be able to tell *how much* force is required for each note, you must therefore notice, always, for every note you play, *how much* the key resists you *before* it gives way and *while it is moving down* under your finger.

You can learn this more easily at first, by trying experiments on three keys together, as in Ex. 3, next page:

Ex. No 3.

Carefully notice *how these keys resist you differently* when you move them slower or quicker. It is very important to be careful in this, for you are here learning one of the most vital laws of playing.

In a word: Never play any note without trying your best to feel exactly *how much* each key resists being moved. If you think thus of *"what each key wants"* this will also make you think of *what the music wants* for each note — and every note may then sound rightly.

Step III: You must now learn to use Arm-weight. Begin thus: Clench your hand lightly into a fist, and then let your fist fall *very gently* upon a black key, or upon two adjacent black keys —

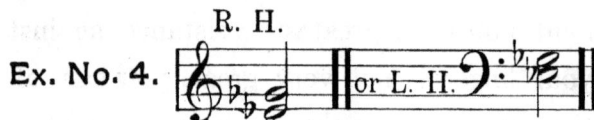

Ex. No. 4.

Let it fall *sideways*, that is, with its soft side (the side opposite to the thumb) turned downwards — with the thumb upwards. When you reach the key and *feel* it, *let* the *whole* go down — the key, the hand and whole arm.

Be most careful not to *make* it go down, but, instead, allow the whole arm (from the shoulder) to be so "easy" and "loose" that its weight just quite gently *weighs* itself down and the key with it. If you do

this correctly, it will seem as if the note "played itself."

Do all this so carefully that the sound is quite the softest the Piano will give you. Afterwards learn to increase the tone to a *forte*, while still using this "Weight-touch," and then decrease it back again to a *pp*.*

Step IV: The next step now is to begin to learn how to use your Forearm "rotatively." Lightly lay your loosely clenched fist on its side as in the last exercise; but here lay it on a table instead of the keyboard. Now gently turn or tilt the fist over, so that the thumb may be brought down to touch the surface of the table. Notice that you do this by a very gentle *twisting* exertion of the Forearm, for you cannot turn the hand without the forearm.

* Remember, you must not in the least, for this kind of touch, seem to *push* the key down with any muscular effort at all, otherwise the note will sound badly, or may even not sound at all. You must here make the sound by thinking solely of a *letting go* of the whole arm — to the extent required by the key's resistance, which you must watch and feel all the time. For if you push *your arm down*, you are making it "stiff." Now no part of you, whether finger, hand or arm, *can be* "stiff" unless you *make it so.* If you make a limb "stiff," this means that you are using *the opposite exertion* as well as the required one, thus giving rise to a "tug-of-war" between the muscles. You can never learn to play properly that way. Everything must always feel perfectly easy, perfectly free, no matter how difficult the passage, or how loud it may be.

Be careful not to twist the Elbow upward.* After you have done this a few times, so as to be able to notice how easy it is, go to the Piano and exercise yourself in sounding together two black keys (or only one) as in *Step III*. But now do so while the hand is in its *rolled-over* position — that which you have just learnt, with knuckles up. And as your fingers are still to be held *gently clenched* (as a fist) you will now reach the keys with the middle "joints" of the clenched fingers — that is, with the under-side of your fist.

Step V: Next, close all the four Finger-tips round the tip of the thumb in a semi-circle, all the nail "joints" bent so as to form a blunt point and all finger-tips reaching the same level, as in Fig. 1. Now continue your "Weight-touch" exercises (*Steps III* and *IV*), but do so on one single black key and with all the finger-tips thus lumped together into a blunt point.

FIG. 1.

When you have learnt to play a key by Weight in this way with some measure of success, then proceed to take a small chord in the same way:

Ex. No. 5.

Play the chord quite softly at first, and afterwards try to increase the tone, without losing sight of the "Weight-touch" process.†

Never forget to make the tone before it is too late. (Re-read *Step I*.) In the meantime you must notice two things: *Firstly*, notice that the three fingers you thus use in playing the chord *are doing some work* as they go down with the keys — for you see they must *exert* themselves sufficiently to enable them to *support* the Arm-weight you are setting free during key-descent; but this exertion may be quite gentle. *Secondly*, notice that you must carefully *adjust* the slight *rotary* exertions of the Forearm, each time, to enable you to play those three notes evenly as to tone.‡

Practise this, as we said before, softly and also loudly — at first use only enough "arm-lapse" to ensure the keys sounding at their softest, afterwards use more weight until you can get quite a *forte*. Try, at once (even in these early stages), to let all weight and force disappear the moment you hear the sound, each time, so that you may *rest* quite lightly on the key-beds after each

this very slight rotary (or twisting) exertion which enables the thumb to reach the table. This exertion should be indeed so slight that you cannot notice it as such, but it must be there all the same.

† Also play different chords, so that your attention, musically, may not flag. Always listen **most** keenly to what you are doing, each time.

‡ That is, the exertions of the fingers and the rotary exertion (and freedom) of the Forearm must exactly balance for each chord you play.

* Notice that the hand will roll back to its fifth-finger side again, *unless you continue in a measure*

sound has been made, and resting with no more Weight than is just sufficient to hold the keys down. Try also, before you make each fresh tone, to judge just how much force is required to overcome the key's resistance.*

Step VI: You must next learn to apply these things to the fingers separately: Start with the Table-exercise of *Step IV*, but after you have rolled the hand over to its playing position, with palm downwards, now *open out all the five fingers* so that the *tips* of all can reach the table. They should be slightly bent, and slightly apart, as if they were over five adjacent keys on the Piano, and the inside of the hand should be so shaped that you could grasp a ball about the size of your fist. Now slightly lift the three "inside" fingers — the index, middle and ring fingers — so that the hand remains resting upon the table, supported by the *fifth* finger and *thumb* only. Next, *rock* the hand by means of the *rotary* motion of the Forearm which you have already learnt,

* As soon as possible learn to play this exercise *Staccato.* (See Step VII.) This means that you must then accurately and *completely* cease *all* force and weight as you reach the sound, so that the keys are thus left quite free to *rebound.* In this form the Exercise should be practised every day, and it in fact forms the most important of the Technical "Daily Tests," as fully described in *"Relaxation Studies,"* Chapter II: "Aiming Exercises"; and as also indicated in *"First Principles,"* pp. 16 and 77.

so that the thumb and fifth finger alternately rise from the table and fall back upon it.

Having learnt this, go to the Piano and do the same there: Place your five fingers over the five adjacent notes C, D, E, F and G, but without sounding these; now notice that to enable you to sound the C and G with your thumb and fifth finger, alternately, you must gently (but sufficiently) *exert* the Forearm in this rotary, twisting or "turning-over" way. You must *first* make this "rotary" exertion to help the *thumb's* exertion in sounding its note, and you must then exactly reverse this "rotary" exertion to help the *fifth* finger to exert itself equally against its key in turn. You will succeed in making these two notes sound with the *same* loudness or softness, provided you are careful to mind these two points: (1) to exert the finger and the Forearm (rotatively) *equally,* and (2) to time those two actions to occur at the same moment — that is, while the key is going down. Practise each hand separately.

Carefully notice that these exertions must be very slight indeed, and that they must last only during key-descent.*

* You may now try to play some tunes, simple enough to be played by the thumb and little finger only, such as the following one. For the left hand, play this two octaves lower.

When you have mastered this process in some measure, you may play with both hands at once, taking the hands two octaves apart so that you may hear each better. At first, however, play the *same fingers* together — while the notes move by contrary motion. It is more difficult at first to play opposite fingers together (with the notes moving by *similar* motion) because the rotary exertions required are then the opposite ones. But you must learn to do this later on.*

Step VII: You must now learn correctly to play STACCATO, and to *"aim"* the act of Tone-production: You have already understood that the only way to make tone is by *moving* the key, and that you must *guide* or *"aim"* all the energy (the force and weight) used, so as to finish this work accurately the moment tone begins.

You must now try to learn to do this more accurately.

* *Note for Teacher:* Also, much later on, the pupil must learn to give these rotary exertions of the forearm (which so much help the fingers) *without showing any motion of the forearm at all*, but, instead, then showing movements of the fingers only. That is, he must then learn to *move* the fingers only, while still giving the necessary rotary *exertions* of the forearm. It only means a slightly different *timing* and adjustment of the finger and forearm exertions relatively to each other. There is no need for him to understand this more difficult matter at present, nor to execute finger movements *without* the actual Forearm movements he has associated therewith so far — time enough later on! For further information see: *" The Forearm Rotation Principle and its Mastery."* (See page 1, Preamble.)

Practise again the chords, etc., as in *Step V;* but now try to *leave off* all force and weight *completely* at the moment of Tone-commencement. If you exactly *time* this ceasing of all energy, and cease it completely, *the keys will be free to rebound*, and the result will be a perfect *Staccato*. Listen most carefully each time for this Staccato, for the sound must be really Staccato — quite dead short. To make sure of this, the keys must be left free to rebound like rubber balls, — it is not enough that they rise *soon after* the sound has commenced, the rebound must be *instantaneous*. This is quite easy, if you do not leave too much Weight to rest on the keyboard, and if you accurately *time* the end of the tone-producing act, as before directed.

While studying this, your finger-tips should *remain upon their keys* while these rebound; else you may fall into the bad habit of trying to *pull* your fingers up when you want Staccato, which is quite wrong.*

In thus learning to play a true Staccato, you are also learning accurately to *"aim"* the act of Touch, for this *never takes longer* than it does in a true Staccato.†

* If you are careful enough to cease all muscular force and weight at the right moment (early enough), the keys are sure to bounce up, even with your fingers and hand lying upon them. Of course if you do not stop *all* Arm-weight, the keys will remain down.

† You can also now learn to do the "Aiming Tests"; *see* "*Relaxation Studies*," p. 9, etc.

Step VIII: (These *Steps, VIII* to *XI,* may be taken now or after *Step XII;* or, better still, *Step XII* may be learnt *in conjunction* with these preceding ones.)

After you have somewhat mastered the true nature of Staccato, you must next try accurately to play *tenuto* and *legato:*—That is, you must now try to learn as accurately to *guide* or *aim* the forces used to make the tone in a *tenuto* as you tried to do in a Staccato. You noticed, when attempting Staccato, that you could not succeed unless you ceased all force and weight accurately enough. Now it is more difficult in tenuto playing than in staccato to detect inaccuracy in tone-aiming. But you should be just as accurate here, else the tone will not sound musical, since it will be either too soft or too loud, which means that the tone will then not be what you intended.

What you now have to learn to do, therefore, each time, after making the sound, is to keep the keys down with only the slightest possible weight that will keep them down. Thus, you must *cease* all the *extra* weight and force which you used *during key-descent* to make the tone; that is, the *tone-making* force must here cease just as accurately and as soon as in Staccato. For instance, if you take the key down with a good deal of Energy (for a *forte*), this energy must immediately vanish once the tone is made, except the little remainder needed to prevent the key from coming up again. In learning this you will also have learnt the next Step, which is:

Step IX: To realize thoroughly, that Tone-making and Tone-sustaining *are two quite distinct things.* You cannot too well keep this in view all through your musical life!

Step X: After you have learnt to understand Tenuto you may try to play *legato.* Legato consists of a close succession of Tenuti, one after the other. But here, instead of merely allowing the light Weight resting on the keys (required to keep them down) to remain on those keys, you must now *pass on* that light weight from note to note (or from finger to finger). This light weight, when thus "passed on," makes a soft Legato seem to the player much like *walking with the fingers*—and you have at the Piano ten legs to walk with!

Moreover, while you must learn thus cleanly to "pass on" the light Weight required to *hold* the notes down (as in Tenuto), you may also, during key-descent (as in Tenuto), use a good deal of Energy to *move* the keys down swiftly, and thus make the sound loud. But such "extra" energy you must *cease accurately* for each note (just as in Tenuto). So you see that between each of the tone-making *acts of touch* (in Legato) you must rest on the key-beds, doing this, however, quite lightly,—in fact, not more heavily than is sufficient to compel the fingers to hold their keys down. In short: a good "natural" Legato depends on your care in doing these two things: (1) Rest very lightly on the key-beds, with just a very little Arm-weight, and see that you transfer this light weight from finger to finger at the right moment; and (2) carefully "*aim*" the *extra* energy needed to make the tone, so that all this *extra* weight and muscular force may accurately disappear the moment you reach each tone, each time.*

Step XI: You will also gradually realize, as you progress further, that when you play a running passage Staccato, you also *here* rest on the keyboard. But *this* "Resting" (in a Staccato passage) must be so light that it can neither take the keys down nor keep them down. In fact, it must be so very light that your hand and fingers now lie loosely on the keyboard, at its surface-level. And this implies that the arm must be so "light," so nicely and loosely *balanced*, that no weight of *it* is left on the keyboard *in between* the sounding of each note. Instead, the weight of the hand, alone, is here left lying on the keyboard.

But remember that to make the sound in Legato, you may use as much Weight and Force each time (during the moment of key-descent) as you have already found necessary to make a *forte* in Staccato and Tenuto.†

* For further details as to "passing on" weight, etc., see pp. 16 and 70, "*First Principles.*" Later on, you must also learn the *artificial* form of Legato. (See "*Commentaries,*" etc., on this point.)

† When your arm thus feels *light* in Staccato, it is not itself resting on the keyboard; instead, it is neatly (but more or less fully) supported by its own muscles. This "self-supported" condition of the arm (you will learn later on) is necessary for all very quick passages, and it is therefore important to learn it as soon as you can.

This "self-supported" (or accurately balanced)

Step XII: You have already learnt to use the thumb and fifth finger separately; in the same way you must now learn to use the remaining fingers separately. To do this you must learn further to understand about "Rotation." You must now learn how EACH finger requires help from those hidden little *rotary* exertions of the Forearm already discussed in the earlier steps. You must learn to give these helpful rotary exertions for each note, and as accurately to *cease* them.

Proceed thus: First rock the hand (as in *Step IV*), playing *C* and *G* alternately with the thumb and little finger, but try to be more and more accurate now, both in the making of each tone and in the "Resting" between each making of the tone. That is, learn accurately to *cease* the work that makes the tone each time, and also learn to make *as light* as it should be that *resting upon the keyboard* which is necessary between each of the tone-makings.

Next, in the same way, rock between the thumb and *ring* finger, but taking a note nearer for the *ring* finger; then do so be-

condition of the arm is at first best learnt away from the keyboard. For instance, hold your arm out in front of you, and imagine that you are "weighing" something with it. Do not be satisfied until you can do this "balancing" really accurately and *freely*. You must not hold nor move the arm stiffly in the least, but must move it gently up and down (a little) so that it feels as if it were *floating in the air*, — so that it feels as if it were just about to drop by its own weight. For further details of such practice, see "*Relaxation Studies,*" Part 2, and "*First Principles,*" pp. 9, 77, etc.

Ex. No. 7.

tween thumb and *middle* finger, and, lastly, between thumb and *index* finger. After having fairly conquered this as a separate exercise for each of these different *fingerings*, finally let the exercise take the above form (Ex. No. 7).

Play this quite slowly at first, and each hand separately; afterwards play the hands together as in the example.*

When you can play the progression from the thumb to any of the other fingers with some ease, then learn to play the reverse progression — from the *little* finger to each of the *other* fingers in turn, including the thumb. So that instead of using the *thumb* as a *pivot* (as in Ex. 7), you now take the

little finger as such a *pivot* from which to make the progression towards the other fingers, musically *as well as rotatively;* see Ex. No. 8, below.

Again practise each hand separately at first, and quite slowly. Afterwards, make these into continuous "five-finger exercises," but do not forget the sense of *progression* all the time (see Ex. No. 9, next page).

You may presently try a far more difficult form of this exercise, and that is, to *play the notes by similar motion* instead of by contrary motion, as you have so far done in *Exs. 7, 8,* and *9.**

* As soon as possible, turn this into a still better exercise, by playing all the *thumb* notes quite softly and all the other fingers considerably louder. This will enable you better to feel that you are playing a *musical progression* each time, from the thumb towards the other finger. Also make it into a little phrase as shown. Also remember the things you were shown in *Steps VIII, IX, X* and *XI.*

* Remember, it is more difficult to play them *properly* by similar motion, because the *rotary* exertions and relaxations of the Forearm, always required, must then be the *opposite* ones in the two hands. This is the reason why it is more difficult to play, with proper *freedom,* a passage in which the notes for the two hands move by similar motion, although it is easy enough to read (or think) the *notes* of such a passage.

When, however, you do proceed to learn to play passages by *similar motion,* it is best, at first, to try

Ex. No. 8.

Ex. No. 9.

You may now learn to play some simple tunes built on the note-progressions you have learnt in *Exs. 7* and *8;* or you may wait until the next *Step* offers you still wider scope.

these *rotatively contradictory* actions between the two hands away from the Piano. Thus: Hold both your arms out in front of you, but somewhat bent at the Elbow, as at the Piano. Now, first turn round (or rotate) both hands from *left* to *right,* as far round as you can easily go — use no violence, but do it swiftly and gently. Then, in the same way, rotate both hands from *right* to *left.* Notice how very likely you are to make these *contrary* movements *stiffly,* unless you are most careful all the time to insist on *freedom* in doing them. Next, practise these rotations while one finger of each hand rests *lightly* on a ledge in front of you. Practise these rotations, in turn, upon all the fingers. It is of course still more difficult to apply these exertions *freely* at the Piano, where you meet the additional difficulty of having to *exert* the required fingers while giving this *rotary* help quite freely and without restraint.

Still, later on, when you have learnt thoroughly to *associate* the rotary exertion with the finger requiring it, you must gradually learn to *reduce* the actual rocking movement you are at present giving for each note. You must then learn to reduce this movement until it is at last hardly noticeable, but you must all the same still thoroughly apply these rotary exertions and cessations you are here learning, although their presence is then hidden from the eye, and although finger-*movements* will then alone be visible.

Such tunes you may play alone, or as a Duet with your teacher. If they are written for your two hands playing the same notes (that is, if the notes move by *similar motion*) you must be very careful to try to remember the things you are just learning as to rotary difficulties when playing passages by similar motion, else you will certainly form bad habits, afterwards difficult to get rid of.

Step XIII: When you have mastered the idea of using the *thumb* or the *little* finger as a pivot for such rotary-and-musical progressions towards any of the other fingers, as shown in the last *Step,* you must next learn to use the remaining fingers similarly as pivots upon which to swing the rotary exertions.

You have already learnt to give such rotary exertions from an *adjacent* finger; for in *Ex. 7* you had to give it from the *thumb* to the *index* finger, and in *Ex. 8* from the *little* finger to the *ring* finger.

You will therefore find no difficulty now in carrying this a step further, and giving these rotary *swings* to assist *each* finger, in turn, from *any* adjacent finger. See Ex. No. 10, next page.

Ex. No. 10

Practise each hand again *separately* at first.

Then play them together as in the Example; and, still later, play the notes by *similar* motion.

Refer to all the advice given under *Step XII.*

Step XIV: When you have thoroughly learnt to make these progressions (musically and rotatively) from each adjacent finger to the next one, you will then be able to apply the rotary *sense*, thus learnt, to a continuous straight-on "five-finger" exercise.

But first, again take this by contrary motion as to notes, so as to give the easiest progression *rotatively* at first. See Ex. No. 11.

In practising this musically simple exercise, be sure to regard it always (both musically and rotatively) as a *progression* from each finger to the next one. That is, you must make it a progression always from a finger which is holding its note *very lightly*, *towards* a finger which has to sound its note quite strongly. This succeeding finger, again, in its turn, after having sounded its own note quite strongly, serves as the *lightly* resting finger-pivot from which still another onward progression is to be made. You thus always progress each time from a muscularly *light* action towards a *stronger* one.

Moreover, the successive notes, thus sounded, again lead on to their little landmarks at the end of each little phrase, etc.*

---

* Once you have mastered the true nature of this simple straight-on five-finger progression, you can easily go further, and learn to apply such *progression from finger to finger* in far more interesting and complicated successions of notes; as an instance, see Ex. No. 12, next page.

Select a few useful ones of this nature from the many to be found in any Piano Primer.

Also, as this will enable you to play *any two notes* in succession within these "five-finger" limits, you

Ex. No. 11

Ex. No. 12

Step XV: All this while you have probably been using more or less pure *third* Species of touch, and more or less actual down-movement of the arm for each note. After you have made considerable progress in the things shown, you must then learn, by degrees, that you can quite easily give the Arm-weight required in such "third species" *without moving the arm at all* up and down, and that you can give it indeed quite well while moving the *finger* only. To enable you to play such "third species" by finger-*movement*, all you have to learn is carefully to *time* the Weight-release of the arm at the right moment and *very slightly* to increase the finger-exertion, and your finger (thus fully supporting the arm) will then carry the key down with the arm-weight, but without showing any arm-*movement*.

Your finger may also reach the key from quite a little distance — an inch or more — and you may still have "third species" *after* you reach the key. If you do not wish your *arm* to move, do not release it until your finger, in its *swing* down, reaches and *feels* the key — that is, *time* the weight to take effect at that moment. In other words, if you exert (or bear up) with the finger, so as fully to support the Weight of the arm at that moment, this Weight will then *not be able to move* down at all, although it is released — and you will thus have "finger-touch" (finger movement) played, if necessary, with *full* arm-weight "behind" it. Of course nearly all this weight (and most of the finger-exertion also) must disappear again as you reach sound in key depression, even in Legato.*

Step XVI: Later on — perhaps a good deal later on — you will also be able to realize that you can play *without* letting go any arm-weight for each separate note. You will find that you can obtain a light

will then be able to play *tunes of much greater musical interest* than were previously possible for you.

It is well also, as soon as possible, to practise all these exercises *Staccato*, as this tests your accuracy in "aiming" tone-production better than does Legato. But remember, in the case of Staccato, that the "Resting" is at the surface level of the keyboard, and that the progression must now, each time, be from a finger which is here resting upon the keyboard *at its surface level.*

* The Swing of the finger *to* the key is quite gentle — not a knock, and there is no stoppage of its movement when you do reach the key; on the contrary, you should continue that movement, but should *add* the right amount of *energy as you feel the key giving way to you.*

* In the same way, a slight change in the balance between the three elements (arm weight, hand-exertion and finger-exertion) may favour that of the *hand,* and we shall then have hand-*movement* (wrist-touch) in place of arm-movement or finger-movement, although the tone is still produced as third *species.*

kind of touch *without releasing the arm at all* — but while leaving it just nicely "balanced," as in the *staccato* form of the "Resting." The tone will then have to be made solely by the exertion of the hand and finger during key-descent — and this we call "*second species*" of Touch-construction.

You can give this "second species" with or without any *visible* sign of the hand's action or exertion in it. That is, you can exert the hand "behind" the finger, while showing a *movement* of the finger, and no movement whatever of the hand.*

Step XVII: So far, also, you have probably been using only one form of finger-movement, and that is the "flat" one. In this the finger, as a *whole*, swings down to the keys and with them — all three "joints" acting in the same direction. It is, in fact, the most usual form of finger-action required, and you may continue using only this one for a long time to come.

* It is also possible to play by using the exertion of the *finger only*. Here the hand lies passive (and inactive) upon the keys, the arm meanwhile being in its "self-supported" state. This we call "*first species*" of Touch-construction. This kind of touch is not very reliable and is but rarely required. But it should be thoroughly understood, since it makes more clear the construction of the others. Pure *second* species, itself, is also comparatively rarely used. In fact you will find, later on, that for quick passages (whether finger or hand movement) one mostly employs *a cross between* "second" and "third" species [*see* page 9, "*Some Commentaries on Pianoforte Technique*" (Longmans, Green & Co.), and page 118, "*Relaxation Studies*" (Bosworth & Co.)] — whereas *pure* "third" species

But presently, when you are more advanced, you must learn how you may also use your fingers in the "bent" way.

The real distinction, here, does not lie in the finger's *shape* at all, but in the two quite different ways in which you may *exert* it, and in the two opposite states of the *upper-arm* which belong to these two kinds of finger-use.

The "flat" finger may be called "clinging" finger. The exertion is in this case inwards, somewhat as in *grasping*, and the *position* of it, when it comes upon the key, may either be *flat* (that is *straight*) or it may also become curved by the time it reaches the key. But when you use the "bent" finger (which may also be called the "thrusting" finger) its motion towards the key is rather that of *unbending* from an already bent position. Therefore, its action against the key is more in the nature of a *thrust*. The action, in this case, is rather

is used almost solely for singing passages, for chords, etc. In any case, you must not try to draw distinctions between these various species in actual playing. Like colours, they must merge one into the other as the passage requires. But you must learn their nature, so that you can *provide* these fundamentals of Piano colouring at will.

At present you need not go further into these matters, but this rough explanation of them will later on help you gradually to understand better " how things are done."

In the meantime try to get your quicker exercises lighter, by not using so much arm-weight, as you probably have done unawares so far. On the other hand, play all your tune notes with real *third* species — *i.e.*, arm-weight separately released for each note.

like that of your leg, when you rise from a chair — you may even notice a slight strain across the knee in doing this; and you may notice a similarly slight *tension* across the "Knee" of the finger when you try to play "bent" finger-touch.

Now notice particularly, when you use such "bent" finger, that its thrust against the key requires also that your *elbow* (and *upper-arm* therefore) are in a slightly *forward* tension at that moment. Therefore, with "bent" finger you cannot have the *whole* arm to help you in making the tone.

In the case of the flat finger, on the contrary, it is the fact of the *whole* arm being released which compels you to use the "clinging" or "flat" finger — because, when you set free the Upper-arm, this tends to draw the hand and fingers away from the Piano, thus causing the *clinging* action of the finger.*

Step XVIII: Till now you have learnt to sound notes only within the "five-finger exercise" compass. You must now extend your Piano-*walks*. You must now learn to make those swift but gentle movements of the Thumb, Hand, and Arm *sideways*

* These matters will at first seem a little difficult to understand. There is no immediate hurry that you should understand them fully. But try as soon as possible to realize how these things *are done* — it will help your progress very much. The Diagrams on the following page (Figs. 2 and 3) may also be of use to you presently.

Fuller details as to these matters are to be found in "*First Principles*" and in "*Relaxation Studies*," etc.

(up and down the Piano), which will enable you to play Scales and Arpeggios, and thus far more interesting tunes, passages and pieces.

To turn the *thumb* "under": Place all five fingers upon five adjacent notes—either at their surface or depressed level. Next, move the *elbow a little* further away from you than it was in the five-finger exercise. Also move the Wrist in the same direction —a little *sideways* and "outwards." You will now find that this will enable your *thumb* to reach notes under the Index, Middle, or Ring fingers (or under the little finger even) without effort.*

Now practise moving the thumb from its own note to these other notes, touching each in turn without sounding them—while the other fingers still remain upon their notes. Allow free *sideway* movements of the hand and wrist to help the thumb in its journey, so that it may not be made "stiff" by going too far under the hand. Let the nail "joint" of the thumb remain nearly in a straight line with its key, whether away from the hand or under it; and be perfectly sure that the movement is perfectly *free* all the time. After this first step, hold down a note by one of the other fingers, and make a little exercise by letting the *thumb* alternately *sound* a note on each side of the one held.

* But to reach "under" with the thumb so far as the little finger you will have to turn your Wrist even more *outwards* than before.

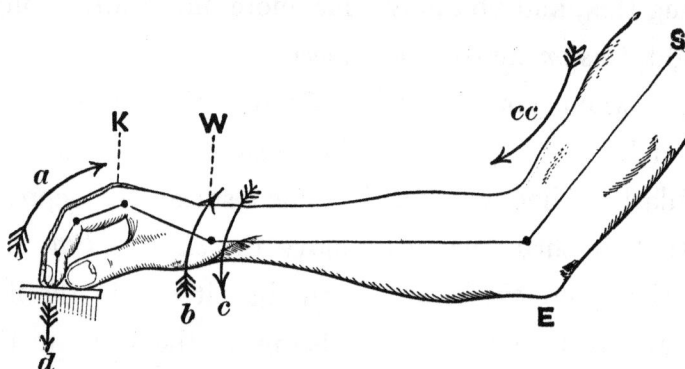

* FIG. 2. — DESCRIPTION: The arrows in the above diagram represent the directions in which the forces tend to act during BENT finger-attitude.

a and b denote the direction of the *reaction* resulting from the *thrusting* action of the finger and hand against the key, and thus reacting upwards and backwards at the knuckle and wrist joints respectively.

c and cc, the energy which balances this, derived from Forearm weight and self-supported Upper-arm.

K is the Knuckle; W the Wrist; E the Elbow, and S the Shoulder.

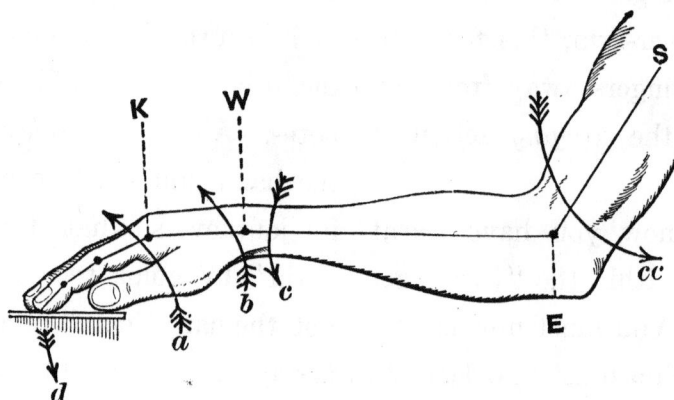

* FIG. 3. — DESCRIPTION: The arrows denote the tendencies during FLAT finger-attitude.

a and b denote the direction of the *reactions* resulting from the finger and hand *clinging* to the key, and how they manifest themselves as an upward and forward-drawing stress at the knuckle and wrist.

c and cc, the direction in which the weight tends to act — the weight of the *whole* arm here, more or less fully released.

d, in both Figs., shows the direction of the total Energy-result, — *vertical* upon the key during its descent, and slightly dragging, in Fig. 3 — " Flat " finger.

* From " *First Principles of Pianoforte Playing*," by kind permission of Messrs. Longmans, Green & Co.

After this, you may then try to play a scale, moving from the centre of the keyboard outwards.*

In learning to pass the thumb under, you have also already learnt to pass the fingers over the thumb. But practise this last also at first as a separate exercise as follows:

To pass the fingers over the thumb: Place your thumb upon a note, either depressed or not, and play notes alternately on each side of it *by the other fingers* in turn. When you have learnt to do this, you will be able to play your *return* Scale with confidence.

Now all this while, never forget the rules as to *Rotation* which have been impressed upon you. But here there is still much more to learn:

When you turn a finger over the thumb, it will at first puzzle you to decide *in which direction* to give the *rotary* help to that finger. There is no difficulty here, if you remember that the rule remains unaltered; that is: that the *direction* of the "Arm-twist" is always *from* the finger which is for the moment acting as a pivot, *towards* the side of the hand to which belongs the finger *you are next going to play with*. Therefore, when you sound a note with a finger which has turned over the thumb, the thumb here acts as the pivot, and the rotary

exertion must hence be towards the *little* finger side of the hand; and this, because relatively to the thumb *all* the other fingers are nearer to the little-finger side of the hand — for this rule holds good, no matter whether the fingers are in their natural position or have been "turned over" the thumb. This is rather a surprise until you see the force of it.*

Be sure, in practising such *lateral* exercises, always to execute the turning over and under perfectly freely. Have your finger ready in good time, and move it into position *gradually*. In playing a scale, you will notice that the *whole* arm (Elbow and all) must travel up and down the keyboard. This motion, also, must always be quite a gentle one, and always quite gradual — without any jerk.†

Step XIX: The Arpeggio hardly comes under "first steps," nevertheless, after the primary steps already dealt with have been overcome, the arpeggio offers little fresh difficulty. The arpeggio only requires still

---

* For further directions on this point and as to learning of Scales and Arpeggios, see "*Relaxation Studies*," page 109, and "*The Act of Touch*," page 299.

---

* There are exceptions to this rule, for instance, when the turning-over finger has to reach very far over. The rule had also better be reversed *when you play double-note progressions* and turn a *long finger over a short one*. But these things do not concern you for a long time yet.

† A number of exercises and fuller details on these points are given in the works previously mentioned. The purpose of practising scales should be to learn to apply the things just pointed out, and to recognize the various fingerings and tonalities. They should never be practised thoughtlessly by the hour.

Ex. No. 13

freer and more ample lateral movements than the scale. Its study should not be delayed too long; anyway, the *preliminary* exercises towards its mastery should be taken up as soon as possible. These preliminary exercises take the form of *groups of arpeggi*. You must practise these, (a) to give you the power to use your fingers freely when these are *extended* over the keyboard; and (b) so that you may again learn to adjust the *rotary* actions under these new conditions. This form of exercise (the arpeggio group) is one of the most useful you can have.

The above is the form of Arpeggio group required (Ex. No. 13 a and b).

Notice that the "pivot" fingers are to be played quite softly — and are to be *held*, while the accented fingers are to give their notes *staccato*. This renders the exercise somewhat more difficult, but very much more useful. Practise all Rotation-exercises on this principle as soon as possible.*

Step XX — As to Position: Sit sufficiently far off from the Piano, so that your

* These, and a large number of others, are found in Chapter IV, "*Relaxation Studies.*"

arm is not bent *square*, but more open than that, thus: ____\ , or ____\ , but not ∟ , otherwise you will find it difficult to apply the weight of the upper-arm.

Have the chair or music-stool of such a height that your *elbow* is not higher than the level of the keyboard — it may be slightly lower. Also, the chair should be midway from the two ends of the keyboard. As to other points, you will find that if you keep to the rules as to the *use* of your fingers, etc., proper positions of hands and fingers will naturally ensue from such correct Condition. Your hand will, *as a consequence*, naturally assume a level position at the keyboard, and your wrist and knuckles will also assume their proper position — about level with each other, or the wrist slightly lower — the fingers, by their action, driving the knuckles of the hand far enough up from the keyboard to enable them (the fingers) to do their work freely. In playing with all five fingers on the white keys, your middle finger should reach its key close to the edge-line of the black keys, the other fingers reaching their notes slightly

* Rotatory difficulties can also be lessened by careful practice of "The Practice Triangle" (Joseph Williams).

behind this point.   The Elbow will also assume its correct position *sideways* if you attend to the rules as to freedom of upper-arm and the rotary necessities of the fore-arm — for the Elbow must *not* be fixed against the side of the body, nor should it be "stuck out" more than is necessary for the sake of such rotary freedom.

Step XXI: A final word, to remind you once again of the most vital thing of all, and that is, never to allow yourself to prac-tise without a keenly felt *musical purpose* for every note you touch.*   You must all

* Insist upon such *rhythmical* purpose even in every scale and exercise you may practise. Feel everything as rhythmical Progression.

HASLEMERE, SURREY, *August*, 1911.

the time *listen* in every sense.   Listen *how* and *when* each note should sound, and listen *to* the sounds as they issue from the Piano. In short: *feel* the Piano-key, so that you may know how much force is required for each note, and listen again so that you may stop the tone-making work "early enough" for each sound, and so that you may give the tone its right Duration — neither too short, nor too long.

Above all things, try to perceive, as soon as possible, that the Music *says Something* to you.   Try to perceive the Feeling and the Poetry the composer wishes to express — through your fingers.

TOBIAS MATTHAY.

APPENDIX

"THE TEACHING OF THE FUNDAMENTALS OF TECHNIQUE TO CHILDREN"

A *Synopsis* of the last portion of a Lecture by Tobias Matthay; first delivered to the
Manchester Teachers' Association in March, 1911.

In the earlier portions of my lecture it was shown how to bring the fundamentals of technique, or playing, before the teacher-pupil, and how this course must be modified to suit the case of the ordinary advanced student who wishes merely to improve his playing powers. We now come to the important question, how the teacher should proceed in the case of children.

In the first instance one must make sure that the child understands the true nature of Music, that he must always look for Rhythm in the sense of *Progression*, and, ultimately, the expression of Feeling when he tries to play — even from the very moment he begins to touch the piano keys. This implies, therefore, a good deal of preliminary training before he is allowed to touch a keyboard — he must have clear notions as to Pulse, and Time sub-divisions, and especially of that idea of Pulse-*growth* into simple musical phrases and sentences which I have been the first to point out, and upon the necessity of which I have for so many years insisted in the case of all pupils, that the basis of all sense of Shape in Music lies solely in the principle of living, rhythmical *Progression or Movement towards definite landmarks*. He must also have learnt to distinguish Pitch-differences, and simple tunes by ear. Then, these things having been accomplished, when you take charge of him at the piano, proceed thus: —

STEP I. — He must first understand the action of the instrument — the action of the hammer, its rebound, and the fact that the continuation of the sound, solely due to the strings' continued movement, is stopped when the damper falls upon them.

The shortness of the act of tone-production, and the uselessness of pressing upon the "key-beds" to make tone must thus be made clear, and the fact that tone depends purely upon key-speed. Make the child himself experiment at the piano on this point.

STEP II. — The facts as to key-resistance, how observed and why observed, are next made clear. Again, the child himself is shown how to experiment on these points.

STEP III. — The production of tone by weight-release is now undertaken, in an elementary form; and with it, therefore, the elision of all contrary-exertion and of arm-exertion. The only logical course is to give this weight-touch, in these first experiments, with the doubled-up hand — as a "fist" held sideways, with thumb up, for we must take only one difficulty at a time.

STEP IV. — Next, to turn the hand over, palm downwards, it will now become clear that rotary-exertion on the part of the forearm is here required. The child must experiment still with his fist, but now with knuckles turned up by means of a slight rotary-*exertion* towards the thumb — but not showing any *movement*, once the hand has been turned into position.

STEP V. — The child will now be ready to attempt a small chord by weight-touch.

STEP VI. — Next, the application of this form of touch to the thumb and little finger, separately, in the form of an elementary rotation exercise, in which these two fingers sound notes alternately.

The child may, in the meantime, be learning to play some tunes, provided they are so constructed as to be playable by these extreme fingers of the hand alone. Or it may prove better to wait until the next few steps have been conquered in a measure.

STEP VII. — The true nature of Staccato must now be inculcated, thus further driving home the fact of the extreme *shortness* of the act of tone-production, and the necessity of its being always carefully "aimed" during key-descent. The necessary elision of weight *in between* the making of the sounds will also here become evident.

STEP VIII. — Properly "aimed" tone-production may next be attempted in *tenuto*.

STEP IX. — The child will now realize that tone-*making* and tone-*sustaining* are two widely different things, always to be kept distinct.

STEP X. — The attempt to learn *legato* may now be made with some hope of success — without risk, as there would be before this, of its leading into all kinds of bad habits.

STEP XI. — The act of Resting, in its two forms of staccato and legato, may now be realized in an elementary form.

STEP XII. — The child has so far sounded notes through thumb and fifth fingers only; he must now learn how the rotary principle applies to *all* the fingers. To do this he must now learn to alternate the Index, Middle and Ring finger with the Thumb, and Little finger.

STEP XIII.—Finally, he must learn to progress *from* any finger *to* any other finger with freedom, because of the proper *rotary adjustments* he is learning to apply.

STEP XIV. — A few strikingly selected five-finger exercises, and *tunes* built on such finger-finger *progressions* will now be available.

Interminable exercise grinding is of course not only useless, but highly to be deprecated from every point of view. Exercise practice is only required for the acquisition of the necessary knowledge as indicated above, and for the acquisition of endurance. Exercise-grinding is quite unnecessary, if the child is taught the facts of rotation, and the other facts of tone-production and duration, and is taught accurately to "aim" every tone from the very first.

Finally, after the child has made some further progress, the other forms of touch-*construction* may, as the opportunity presents itself, be explained to him, and learnt — as up to this point only *third* "*species*" has been used. Also, as a further step onward, he must learn those side-to-side movements of the hands, fingers and thumb, and of the arm, which will enable him to play a scale. Also, as the opportunity occurs, he may be shown how he can *move* a finger only, while nevertheless applying arm-weight — a matter not difficult for a child to understand, although often difficult for its elders, who have mislived their years with upside-down notions of "Touch." Thus, the child will also by degrees learn to realise the important distinction between touch-*construction* and its mere accompanying movement. Later on, he must also learn to distinguish between *flat* and *bent* methods of finger-use, with their correlated states of the upper-arm. Or an opportunity of showing him this distinction may already have arisen, incidentally. As soon as possible also, after the scale-playing stage has been reached, the child should begin the study of broken chords — "groups of arpeggi," starting here with a close application of the rotary principle to every note, as explained in my "*Relaxation Studies*," etc., thus gradually bringing within his grasp the arpeggio positions, and correlated lateral adjustments of the hand and arm.

Points as to position (of the body itself, distance from the instrument, etc.) will also by this time have naturally arisen. All these points, it will be noted, will have arisen *as a means to effect the production of Music* itself by the child — to enable the child to fulfil his wish to *hear* and to *make* actual Music. Remember, this is the fundamental, vital, ever-powerful teaching-principle to keep in view throughout. It must indeed be ever kept in view whether teaching children or their elders, — none must ever be allowed to forget, even for a moment, that the purpose must ever be *to make music*, or *to enable other people to make it*, or *to enable others and ourselves to perceive it*.

TOBIAS MATTHAY

PUBLISHED

PIANOFORTE MUSIC

Four Novelletten—Op. 1	(FORSYTH BROS.)	8/- complete
Nocturne in D flat—Op. 3 (new edition)	(EDWIN ASHDOWN)	4/-
Hommage à Chopin—Op. 4	(FORSYTH BROS.)	4/-
Seventeen Variations—Op. 5	(FORSYTH BROS.)	4/-
An Autumn Song—Op. 6	(FORSYTH BROS.)	3/-
*In Spring Time (Three Miniatures)—Op. 7	(ANGLO-FRENCH CO.)	5/- complete
*A Summer Day Dream—Op. 8 (new edition)	(ANGLO-FRENCH CO.)	2/-
A Waltz Whim—Op. 9 (new edition)	(ASCHERBERG)	4/-
In Winter—Op. 10 (new edition)	(ASCHERBERG)	4/-
Moods of a Moment (ten numbers)—Op. 11 (new edition)	(ANGLO-FRENCH CO.)	6/- complete
Love-Phases (Minnelieder) (three numbers)—Op. 12 (new edition)	(JOSEPH WILLIAMS) complete 3/- net
Monothemes (six numbers)—Op. 13	(FORSYTH BROS.)	3/- net
Lyrics—Op. 14 (seven numbers)	(PATERSON)	2/-
Scottish Dances—Op. 15 (four numbers)	(PATERSON)	4/-
Prelude from Suite of Studies—Op. 16 (new edition)	(ANGLO-FRENCH CO.)	2/-
Intermezzo in E, from Suite of Studies—Op. 16	(RICORDI)	1/6 net
Bravura (Finale), from Suite of Studies—Op. 16	(RICORDI)	2/- net
Elves—Op. 17 (new edition)	(WEEKES & CO.)	2/-
Con Imitazione—Op. 18	(WEEKES & CO.)	2/-
Romanesque—Op. 19 (new edition)	(WEEKES & CO.)	2/-
Toccata—Op. 21	(ANGLO-FRENCH CO.)	2/-
*Dirge, from Stray Fancies—Op. 22	(ANGLO-FRENCH CO.)	1/6
*Albumblatt, from Stray Fancies—Op. 22	(ANGLO-FRENCH CO.)	2/-
From my Sketch Book. Book I.—Op. 24 (five numbers) (ANGLO-FRENCH CO.) Complete 5/- net cash
Separately : No. 2, 'May Morning'; No. 5, 'Terpsichore'	2/- each net cash
By my Fireside—Op. 25 (five numbers)	(JOSEPH WILLIAMS) Complete 3/- net cash
From my Sketch Book. Book II.—Op. 26	(ANGLO-FRENCH CO.)	5/- net
Separate : Nos. 2 and 5, 1/6 net ; No. 6, 2/- net
Mood Phantasy—Op. 27	(JOSEPH WILLIAMS)	5/-
31 Variations on original theme in A major and minor—Op. 28	(AUGENER)	5/- net
*Five Cameos for Miniature Players—Op. 29	(ANGLO-FRENCH CO.)	3/- net
On Surrey Hills (five numbers)—Op. 30	(ANGLO-FRENCH CO.)	4/-
Three Romantic Pieces (Ballade ; Duetto ; Mazurka)—Op. 31	(ANGLO-FRENCH CO.)	2/- each
Summer Twilights (four numbers)—Op. 32	(ANGLO-FRENCH CO.)	4/-
Three Lyric Studies—(Op. 33)	(ANGLO-FRENCH CO.)	3/-
Toccata, No. 2, in F (Moto Perpetuo)—Op. 34	(ANGLO-FRENCH CO.)	3/- net
*Playthings for Little Players (Ten Studies)—Op. 35	(ANGLO-FRENCH CO.)	3/- net
Toccatina in D (Study in Double Notes). Book I—Op. 36	(ANGLO-FRENCH CO.)	2/6 net
*First Solo Book (Nine Little Pieces)—Op. 37	(ANGLO-FRENCH CO.)	2/6 net
*Playthings for Young and Old. Book II. (Eight pieces)—Op. 38	(ANGLO-FRENCH CO.)	3/- net
Ballade in A minor—Op. 39	(ANGLO-FRENCH CO.)	3/- net
Cadenzas to Beethoven's Concerto, No. 1, in C, Op. 15	(AUGENER & CO.)	2/6 net

*Children's and easy music ; the order of difficulty is Op. 37, Op. 35, Op. 38, Op. 29
Op. 7, Op. 8, and Dirge Op. 22

FOR PIANOFORTE AND VIOLIN

A Pamphlet—Op. 2	(EDITION CHANOT)	4/-

FOR PIANOFORTE AND STRINGS

Quartet in one movement—Op. 20	(ANGLO-FRENCH CO.)	5/- net

FOR PIANOFORTE AND ORCHESTRA

Concert-Piece, No. 1 in A minor (Concerto in one movement)—Op. 23	(RICORDI)	
SOLO, with orchestral accompaniments arranged for a 2nd pianoforte		5/- net
String parts		each 1/- net

MS. full score and wind parts, etc., on hire from the publishers.

www.ingramcontent.com/pod-product-compliance
Lightning Source LLC
Chambersburg PA
CBHW052331100426
42737CB00055B/3361